WHAT'S IN A NAME

The Power of Becoming

A Tau Lady Anthology Written By:

Kim Arrington, Michelle Dixon, Damita Wynn,

Stacie Hayes, Raychelle Lee, Korean V. Peoples,

Cherise Lenore Riley, Nyree Dawn Fray and Erika Lee

ISBN: 978-1-954595-16-3

Printed in the USA
Duncanville, Texas

Library Congress Control Number: 2022904182

Published by Sparkle Publishing
www.sparklepublishing.net

Sparkle Publishing
Write. Publish. Sparkle.

Table of Contents

Introduction

"Death and life are in the power of the tongue,
and those who love it and indulge it will eat
its fruit and bear the consequences of their words."

(Proverbs 18:21 Amplified)

Did you know that your tongue is the deadliest weapon ever created in the entire existence of mankind? You are probably wondering what I mean by that because there are way more weapons in the world that are deadlier than the tongue. Well, in theory, there may be deadlier weapons; however, the tongue is the only weapon created that can take life and give life. We use our tongue to create words, and words have the power to create and shape our reality or false sense of reality. Think about it this way – have you ever awakened and did not want to get out of bed, and then subconsciously began to think to yourself, "I hate this day" or "this is going to be a bad day"? If we are honest, the majority of us, if not all, have had those thoughts and said those words.

1

Now think about that day; Bad things happened, but why?

Because our words gave power to our thoughts, and we began speaking it out of our mouths and believed it in our hearts. That is the power of the tongue.

Think about a time when you went about your day and only spoke positive things, and I do not mean just saying them to say them, but really believing them. I bet your day was filled with joy, and if bad tried to come, the environment you created with what you released from your thoughts and tongue placed a shield around you, keeping your posture toward the good thing and not focusing on the potential bad.

"For as he thinks in his heart, so is he."

(Proverbs 23:7 NKJV)

At some point, we have heard the age-old saying first reported in 1862: "Sticks and stones may break my bones, but words will never hurt me." The reality is, this saying is a half-truth. Yes, sticks and stones may break your bones, but words definitely have the power to hurt you. Words shape our identity, and our identity tells us who we are, and based on who our identity tells us we are, will determine the paths we take in life. These paths can lead to an abundant life or a life full of pain, misery, hurt, and regret. Most identities are falsely created by words spoken over us that gave birth to horrible situations and circumstances. Think about the person abandoned at an early age. Abandonment gives birth to "not being good enough" or "not worthy of love." Those statements can send a person down a path with the belief that they are not good enough or worthy of love, causing them to spend years battling rejection which can lead to bad decision making, toxic relationships, dead end jobs, and one-sided friendships.

Why?

Because they are spending their time trying to prove to others that they are good enough.

We allow words to tell us who we are, and we end up falling in alignment with those words, even when those words are far away from our true identity in Christ.

We were never created to live based on a lie.

So, what is a lie?

A lie is an untrue statement with intent to deceive.

Circumstances and perceptions are known for creating untrue statements about our lives and destiny to deceive us into believing that is who we are or why we were created. The reality is you were created for so much more, and understanding who you are and awakening to your true identity will unlock a power you never knew existed. This power will create the world you were purposed and destined for. This power will remove the shackles of doubt, fear, and unbelief, causing you to walk in boldness as you take back your authority, declaring the true identity of who you are and whose you are.

For many, this will be a process, but I want you to know it is never too late to start. Regardless of where your journey has taken you, as long as you have breath in your body, you have another opportunity to get back on the right path toward discovering exactly who you are and the power of your name in order to become! Your name holds weight, more weight than you know, and until you get to the root of it, you will not have the awakening you need to possess the power and authority that comes with it.

Jesus knew the importance of knowing exactly who He was because who He was tied directly to His purpose and destined assignment on this Earth. But more powerfully, those who walked with Him were able to tap into His true identity because He knew who He was and was unshakable in it. Matthew 16:13-17 (NIV) shows us the blessing in this:

When Jesus came to the region of Caesarea Philippi, he asked his disciples, "Who do people say the Son of Man is?" They replied, "Some say John the Baptist; others say Elijah; and still others, Jeremiah or one of the prophets." "But what about you?" he asked. "Who do you say I am?" Simon Peter answered, "You are the Messiah, the Son of the living God." Jesus replied, "Blessed are you, Simon son of Jonah, for this was not revealed to you by the flesh and blood, but by my Father in heaven."

What names or words (failure, dumb, not good enough, unlovable, etc.) have you spoken over yourself or allowed others to speak over you? As you read each chapter, my prayer is that every story of discovering the power of a name and the power to become will usher you onto the path of your true identity. I pray that you discover the power that already resides on the inside of you, waiting to be unlocked, uncovering layer by layer to feel the impact and weight that your name (words) holds as you allow the Holy Spirit to uproot every name (word) spoken over your life that does not align with who you truly are or your God-purpose and destiny. I pray that He seals every wound that was created, even the hidden ones that still exist, while preventing your scars from reopening or hindering you on your journey.

"I will give thanks and praise to You, for I am fearfully and wonderfully made; Wonderful are Your works, And my soul knows it very well."

(Psalm 139:14 Amplified)

Michelle Dixon

Alias; Teresa Ann Logan

Michelle "In-Sightful" Dixon

"Luck of the draw or meant to be? Our lives are impacted by forces that we cannot explain, often changed for reasons we will never totally understand. However, when people are touched by the hand of fate, they know it. Whether fate brings them their hearts' desire or forever closes the door to their dreams, the path that brought them to that point is clear, and fate's irony is unmistakable."

(Thomas Wilson)

For the first three months of my life, I lived under the assumed name of Teresa Ann Logan. We all know the standard procedure that occurs in naming babies when they are born. So, how does a three-month-old baby have an alias?

Let me explain.

I was born and placed in an orphanage utilized by unwed mothers, and I lived there for three months under the alias of Teresa Ann Logan. My birth mother's name was Teresa Ann Logan, and even though she could not or did not give me a home, she gave me her name and moved on.

A married couple by the name of Ernest and Betty Hudson came to the orphanage in hopes of adopting a baby boy to quell the heartache and disappointment of several miscarriages. Their hope that becoming parents would also shore up the deterioration of their seven-year union.

When I share the truth of my life experiences, something I have always shared is that my adopted parents picked me out the same way one might pick a puppy from a litter. Remember that the goal was to pick out a bouncing baby boy to take home and fill the void of loss and to help Ernest and Betty feel more complete in their peer group. After all, their next-door neighbors who were my father's childhood friend and buddy, whom he enlisted in the navy with, were the proud parents of three with another one on the way. So, walking away from the orphanage with a child would "normalize" them within their peer circle.

The layout of this orphanage as I have been told was a vast open room with multiple bassinets, cribs, and playpens to hold the babies and accommodate their various stages of development. Ernest and Betty's focus was to find a baby boy.

I am told that my crib was on the very back wall in the corner of this room. I'm not sure, and I have often wondered how many cribs and baby boys Ernest and Betty surpassed to arrive at my crib. The story goes that I was laying in my crib on my back, cooing, giggling, blowing spit bubbles, and playing with my feet, totally entertained in my own world. Betty looked down into my crib and exclaimed, "Oh, Butch!" to which my father silently responded in his head, "Ahh, shit!"

"Go ahead, if you just got to have her," he said to his wife.

Back to my earlier thought of picking out a baby like you pick a puppy—usually, the most rambunctious or energetic puppy does whatever to get noticed and is usually selected. So, whether a coincidence, fate, or luck of the draw that day, Alias, Teresa Ann Logan, would become known as Michelle Louise Hudson and would no longer reside in an orphanage.

My father decided to name me after a niece he had except he insisted on spelling my name with two Ls. My middle name, Louise, was given to me by Betty because it was her middle name and she hated it yet gave it to me. Michelle is the feminine derivative of Michael. In Hebrew, Michael translates to "who is like God" or "close to God." Louise is the feminine derivative of Louis which translates to a famous warrior or well-known fighter. A namesake of being close to God and a well-known fighter would serve me well in surviving, evolving, and understanding my identity in God while growing up in the Hudson household.

Sometimes, the right thing can be done but for the wrong reason, the right thing being a home and a sense of belonging for an orphaned child. However, the sole reason to adopt a child is to love and give a child a home, not to "fix" underlying issues in a relationship, appease your spouse, and "keep up" with your peer circle. Ernest and Betty Hudson were married seven years by the time the decision was made to look into adoption. But the bottom line was they really did not know each other or how to communicate effectively. There were also underlying emotional issues and a problem with alcohol on both sides. I often wondered how they were allowed to adopt, but I was placed in their custody and became the apple of my father's eye while I watched in confusion and felt my mother's growing resentment toward me.

My parents told me I was adopted before I entered kindergarten so that I would know and be prepared for the cruel things that children sometimes hear and repeat from adults. I was and never have been insecure about being adopted. My insecurity stemmed from a growing awareness that my mother did not like me, and I was not even sure that she loved me. So, I started asking myself the question around age 12, "What makes me so unlovable that two mothers don't or can't love me?" What an awful burden for a child to carry, and I carried that burden far into adulthood and allowed it to shape critical decisions in my life. Growing up under the constant barrage of criticism and verbal abuse from a mother who constantly reminded me that I was not enough, not pretty enough, not light enough, my hair texture was the wrong texture, and I believed I embarrassed her. I was an extremely nervous child who walked on eggshells, anticipating the next "wrong" thing that I would do to set off my mother. So, anything or any place that was not home became my sanctuary, especially church. People have remarked all my life that I am an old soul, wise beyond my years.

God revealed Himself to me at an early age and still speaks to me in dreams. No matter how terrible things got in my home life, I believed that God was always with me and that I could endure whatever came my way. But God, I have survived beatings that should have left me with permanent damage. I had a bleeding ulcer at the age of 11 due to the stress of trying desperately to understand why I was rejected as a daughter. Even though I went through a period when I wanted to die, and I felt that it was a mistake I was born, that small place in my heart that God occupied and constantly encouraged let me know that better days were coming, there was a purpose for my pain, and that I was His daughter. I knew I could not give up the teachings of Christ I was learning in Sunday school and church.

I gave my life to Christ at the age of 13. Shortly after, a tornado tore through our town and destroyed everything. I realized I did not want to die not knowing Christ as my Savior. During this time, I continued to pray and ask God to show me how to love and honor my mother and to make her proud of me. Then came a miraculous move of God. Isaiah 61:3 talks about "beauty for ashes." God will see our tears and heartache and He will turn sadness into joy. Shortly after I was baptized, my mother re-dedicated her life to God. She stopped drinking and started serving God. The following year, in 1975, my father gave his life to Christ, stopped drinking immediately, and started serving God. Both parents were alcoholics that drank daily. My father was a federal employee and drank before work, at lunch, and after work. Neither of them ever went to AA or rehab, yet they stopped immediately and never drank alcohol again until they transitioned to eternal rest. My mother died in 1986, one month after I had my third son. Our relationship never got to where I thought it should be, but we tried. My father died in 2009, and it was devastating because he was my rock. But life has taught me to trust God completely. This man that wanted a boy, and who was not thrilled in seeing I was the final selection, changed my name from an alias to a name that means close to God. My father's amazing testimony was how he had four nervous breakdowns over his lifetime that required hospitalization and heavy tranquilizers. He testified how a demon sat on his bed one night and showed him his entire life and told him he would kill him before he was 45 years of age (he was 45 when he gave his life to Christ). He testified that he knew and understood "why" he adopted me. He said it was in God's plan for me to be adopted into his household because God used me to lead him and my mother to Christ.

Beauty for ashes, God will give us when we trust Him.

My destiny and divine order are to live close to God and be a warrior for Christ to lift His name so that others will be drawn to Him.

I started this life as Teresa Ann Logan, but my identity and destiny are Michelle Louise Hudson-Dixon, but even as my sorors call me by my God-given line name, "In-Sightful," I continue to grow and evolve. The Scripture attached to my God-given name is Proverbs 4:4-7 (NKJV):

He also taught me, and said to me: "Let your heart retain my words; Keep my commands, and live. Get wisdom! Get understanding! Do not forget, nor turn away from the words of my mouth. Do not forsake her, and she will preserve you; Love her, and she will keep you. Wisdom is the principal thing; Therefore get wisdom. And in all your getting, get understanding.

I thank God for everything He has allowed me to overcome.

Erika Lee

Can You See Me?

Erika Lee

When you see a person addicted to drugs, they are often called a "crack head." When you see a person walking down the street, talking out loud to themselves, they are often called "crazy". When we see an overweight person, they are often called "fat." When you see a little girl that looks grown-up, older than her actual age, she is often called "fast tail." But why do we see something or someone and immediately rename them?

It's funny how people never really see you. They only see the you they want to see. They don't see the smoke that caused the fire to make you who you are. They don't see the older cousins who took your innocence and virginity. They see a promiscuous girl, a fast-tail gal. They don't know that you still cry at night because you don't know why you had to grow up early and all the family could say was "she's too grown." But why was she too grown? No one took the time to find out why? Why do we make a judgment before we know anything?

I was the oldest girl in the family. I was a sickly baby. Many doctors did not think I was supposed to live (that's my momma's testimony), but I did live! I've been beating the odds set against me since I was born. I was born with an illness that only premature babies or male babies were born with. I was neither. I was only given until the age of three to live. Today, I am well over 40. I was told because of intestinal damage that I would never have kids, yet I birthed two healthy sons. I have been beating the odds set against me all of my life. But there was a forgotten odd. I was a female who bloomed early. I had a full set of breasts by the age of 11 years old. Yes, I was top-heavy early. My waist was small, but my legs and thighs were not. I was considered "thick" or fat as the old folks would say. And because I bloomed early, people thought I was older than I was. I had the responsibility of being older and the attitude of being older. I walked and talked like I was older. So, I started lying about how old I was. And if you didn't know, you didn't know.

But why?

But why is a question no one ever asked me—why is she acting older, why is lying to be older?

Nope, they just called me a fast-tail gal. No one took the time to see me.

I was the oldest girl in the family. My mom had five kids. I have one older brother, and then it's me. My mom had three more kids with my bonus dad. But that's not it. My grandmother had six children and each of those six kids had kids. I was the oldest girl. My auntie had four kids, and we were all raised close together, sometimes in the same house. When the holidays came around, all the other kids got to go play. I got to go into the kitchen and cook. Then, I had to clean. Oh, and the night before, I had to do hair. Nope, not my hair, but all the girls' hair in the family. At the time, I didn't know it was a problem. It was the life I was used to living.

My mom was sick for almost five years straight. Her husband worked all the time. My bonus dad always kept a job. He has to be the hardest working man I have ever known. This left the responsibility of the younger three children to me. I cooked, cleaned, bathed the kids, and combed hair. I was the bonus mom for a lack of better words. Then, God healed my mom, and she was so thankful to be healed. She went all over the world preaching the Gospel. She had five children and a husband, but her oldest daughter, me, was assumed to handle things. She didn't know any better. Then, my auntie got sick, and my grandma added more responsibility to my plate, instructing me to help with my three younger cousins. And they each had lots of hair. But again, no one knew what being the oldest meant to me or what it was doing to me. I asked them why me in a nice way, of course. My family is from the slap-a-kid era, so I knew to tread lightly with my questions of why.

"You're the oldest."

"Ask God, He made you first."

When the holiday time came around and all the family got together, updating each other of their lives and kids' lives, they would call me fast tail.

The night I overheard this conversation changed my world forever, the night I heard my family call me "fast tail." I was 14 years old and went from fast tail to rebelling overnight. I went from being the dependable one, who would take care of everything and everybody, to not caring about anyone, not even myself. I cried that night, wondering why they kept calling me fast. I was beginning the second semester of my 9th-grade year at Hamilton High School. And I became a force to reckon with. You couldn't tell me anything. I was determined to show them what fast tail was.

Pause, let's go back.

My entire family was big. We had a set of cousins that would come from St. Louis every summer to Milwaukee just to visit. We loved being together. Either they were coming to Milwaukee or we were going to St. Louis. This happened every summer until I was about 13 years old. But one of my cousins who was about three years older than I was, decided it was time I grew up. He decided we were going to play house. He decided we would play husband and wife, only I was his cousin, and I was 12 years old. I knew nothing about sex. I knew nothing about sperm. I was 12 years old. And back in those days, the older folks didn't talk to kids about sex. I was 12 years old, and my cousin got behind me, lifted my skirt, pulled down my panties, and inserted his manhood into me. I didn't know what was happening, so I asked him questions. He said to hold up, and it's okay just be still. Then when he was finished, he put his findings on my back, and I asked what was that? He said it was nothing and wiped it off with my blanket. Then, he turned around and went out the door. I sat there confused for a minute, feeling lost. This continued to happen every year until I was 16. I stayed away from him or I made sure to never be alone with him. The older I got, the more I learned. I would soon learn what was what. But still, I never said anything. That was my cousin. Was it wrong? Was I supposed to tell someone? Who was I supposed to tell? I didn't know. But I do know they started calling me fast tail. Every family gathering, I was hearing how fast I was acting, but who was protecting me? Who noticed that something had happened to me?

During year 13 of my life, it wasn't my cousin who would abuse me. It was our cousin's brother on her mama's side. He was way older than me, at least 13 years older than me. He thought it was a good idea to stick his hands down my pants every time he saw me. He thought my vagina was his playground. Every time I went over there, he would find a way to corner me and get a good feel of me. How was I to know this was also considered sex? No

19

one told me. The older I got, he would take my hand and put it down his pants. I had never seen a grown man's penis before until he pulled his out and placed it inside of me. Well, by then, I was used to someone putting their penis on me and in me. But who noticed my silence? Who noticed the cries in me? Who noticed me? No one. They just called me "fast tail" and kept moving.

People saw the smoke but didn't see the fire. They saw my attitude had changed. They saw my hips had spread. They saw my body had changed. But they didn't see me. People get so caught up in what they see that they forget it's a story to go with that. They forget there's smoke before the fire. We see the outside of a person and form opinions without learning facts.

What's in a name? Crazy, crackhead, fat, fast tail? All are names of opinions. Those names were created out of someone's opinion. Until I was grown, I didn't realize I had been molested by a loved one. Until I was grown, I didn't realize that my family didn't see me for who I was. Until I was grown, I didn't realize that shouldn't have happened to me. Until I was grown, I didn't realize that it continued because I didn't speak up. Until I was grown, I didn't realize it wasn't my fault. I accepted being called fast tail until I rebelled. Then they called me rebellious and fast tail gal.

At 15, I had two different penises in my vault, and neither was of my own doing. I had been called "fast tail" long enough. I started to break out on my own. The first person I willingly agreed to open my vault to was in the back of the church. Yes, the back of the church, I was supposed to be at Sunday school, but I was in a closet. He was older, he had liked my best friend, and had gotten another girl in the church pregnant. But he liked me. My self-esteem was non-existent because someone took my virginity at an early age. Someone in my family took my self-esteem and left me with none.

I was called fast tail so much that I leaned into the word and became fast tail for real. By the age of 16, I had three different penises in my vault. And none loved me. They saw the big boobs and hips and spread my legs wide.

What's in a name? There comes a time in everyone's life that they have to decide will this be the thing that makes me or will this be the thing that breaks me. Will you allow this to be the thing that defines you, defines your vision, defines the way you walk, talk, believe, or will it cripple you? Will it keep a hold on your life and make your life miserable because you won't let it go? I was watching a famous stage play, and I heard them say that it's not why they call you but what you answer to. That was a defining moment in my adult life. That was the moment I realized I didn't have to be what others have called me. I was not a fast tail gal. I was not mean. I was not stuck up. I was, however, on a journey to self-discovery to finding out what's in a name, what I would answer to, and what I allowed to define me.

I was packing to move again. Yes, I was a single mother who, unfortunately, had to move around a lot. I worked low-paying jobs and lived in a high-priced area to make sure my boys had the best education I could give them. I lived in the suburbs, but my bank account said I should be on section eight for assistance. But as I was packing up, I saw a few old journals I had written in. I had been journaling for as far back as I can remember. Only back in the 80s, it was called writing in your diary. I found myself reliving the pain, nursing what I had already grown through. Then, I found myself reading the journals and reading the Bible at the same time. And what my momma had spoken to me years ago when I couldn't hear her, started to replay in my head: "God has a plan for your life"; Jeremiah 29. God didn't let you live without having a purpose for your life. I remember when she said that when others give up on you, God knows what He is doing.

As I replayed my mom's words, read my journal, and read the Bible, I heard God say, "It's time now." It was as if I could hear Him clear as day tell me it's time to give Him my life, heart, pain, and my all. I had done everything I was big and bad enough to do. I had done everything against the Word of God. I had gone against all of the ten commandments, including the one commandment He gave us in the New Testament. God called me into action. He said, "It's time you answered to who I called you to be." He reminded me of the Scripture that said I am fearfully and wonderfully made.

I said, "God, I can't see how I am beautiful when I have done so many ugly things." God said in His Word, "Your faith has made you whole."

I had done too much, but I was still going to church. I couldn't see my way out. I couldn't see the beauty in me that God sees in me. I began to read the words of God. He said in His Word to be of good cheer, your sins are forgiven. In Matthew chapter 9, he said to arise, take up your bed (bed equals to hurts, habits, and hang-ups), and go to your house (house equals His throne); lay your burdens at My feet.

The tears would fall for days, weeks, and months. I slowly began to see myself as God sees me. I no longer answer to the pain. I answered to the compassion and love of Jesus. I soon learned not to let anyone tell me or make me feel less than. Now, when I speak, I no longer hear the pain. People wonder how I am always on a good vibe. It's the love of Jesus. I can now answer to who I am in Him. I had to fight to become the woman I am today. I now know I am not breaking; I am not broken but unfolding every day. I realized I have survived what I have been through.

If someone calls you your pain, remember that you don't have to answer it. You can walk on by. You can heal from what broke you. Start by writing it down. Then read it, burn it, rip it, delete it, and just plain get rid of it. Now open your Bible and read what God calls you. Next, write the vision. Write what you want your life to be. Map out a plan on how to get there. Pray, plan, and execute daily to live your dream life. You are who God says you are, and He calls you BELOVED!

Kim Arrington

Unbr8kable!

Kim Arrington

Wow, and just like that, it's finished. The doctor called it—time of death: 10:00 am, Sunday, December 27, 2021. At that moment, I was truly naked, unashamed, and unmasked, testing my faith and the raw truths of whose hand was I really holding, whose voice was really guiding me, and the purpose I was pursuing. Dad represented my recovery, strength, measured milestones of success, and confirmed my identity. It took a long time for me to get to this place of loving me, Kim Denise, to the woman staring back in the mirror.

"And in Christ you have been brought to fullness. He is the head over every power and authority."

(Colossians 2:10 NIV)

I was a young girl, lost between two worlds, growing up in white suburbia and typically the one out of five Black girls in school. My parents were so proud of their blessing to raise their child in a better environment, giving thanks to God for all He blessed their hands to prosper. I worshipped in our home church, Mt. Zion Baptist Church, in Newark, New Jersey, the inner city, truly urban America. I worshipped and was bullied by the Black girls in the youth group, all of who found me to be less than good enough to fit in. I allowed their words of "you sound like a white girl," "you dress like a white girl," and "nobody wants you around" to hurt me. I wore those words of shame and felt like I was never good enough to fit in. I navigated young adulthood by putting on the I-am-okay mask. What I did find was that I fit in with the older boys. Well, they were men, and they appreciated me. I was smart but not sure I was super pretty. I later reflected I was just dumb because what I traded for their attention and acceptance almost cost me a lifetime.

"I no longer call you servants, because a servant does not know his master's business. Instead, I have called you friends, for everything that I learned from my Father I have made known to you."

(John 15:15 NIV)

"But he said to me, 'My grace is sufficient for you, for my power is made perfect in weakness.' Therefore I will boast all the more gladly about my weaknesses, so that Christ's power may rest on me."

(2 Corinthians 12:9 NIV)

The party life came with drugs, alcohol, and regrets. I often snuck out and lied about my whereabouts, such as high school prom, when I actually was with my forbidden boyfriend. I experienced a short stint at college in Ohio, but I was flying back and forth to Newark, New Jersey, on weekends, all expenses paid by this forbidden love of my life. Within a year, it all came crashing down. My college uninvited me back the next year, and my dad made it clear that I had two choices—college and he would pay for it or start me off in life whether an apartment or trade school. Since I had already selected college and bombed out of school, I was now on my own to figure out this next chapter in life. I surely was not going to let the folks at home know I failed. I simply had to adjust the mask. In Philippians 1:12, Paul speaks of what happened to me is for the furtherance of the Gospel, that God's Testimony is in the making: *"Now I want you to know, brothers and sisters that what has happened to me has actually served to advance the gospel"* (Philippians 1:12 NIV).

The mask hid my shame, and I relied on it as a coping mechanism for the hurt, insecure little girl inside. I continued using drugs, but they were no longer a weekend party thing. I found myself on binges that lasted days. I lost a job because I passed out at work and was crawling around the house because I was so paranoid someone would see me in the window, which drove me to call 9-1-1. I actually called the suicide hotline for help and was placed on hold. I was listening to music and hearing my heart racing. By the time they came back on the line, I started coming down from my high and was able to ask for help. I attended my first Narcotics Anonymous (NA) meeting that night.

"He restoreth my soul: He leadeth me in the paths of righteousness for his name's sake."

(Psalm 23:3 KJV)

I married at 21 years old to my husband, 19 years my senior (smile), and life seemed grounded. We quickly found it challenging to have children, and I had to reflect whether this was a consequence and fruit of my past actions. I heard a pastor say that sometimes you can make mistakes that can't be fixed so easily. You sow that seed of disobedience, and while God releases forgiveness, one may have to eat the fruit of their harvest.

Adoption allowed us to create a family, and we moved forward. One year into parenting, I found myself pregnant.

A miracle?

Some would say so.

God will restore the years the cankerworm destroyed.

"Be strong and very courageous. Be careful to obey all the law my servant Moses gave you; do not turn from it to the right or to the left, that you may be successful wherever you go."

(Joshua 1:7 NIV)

Living beneath my privilege and my family, He continued to walk by my side, thanks to His Grace. I found myself rededicating my life to Christ. With a Holy Ghost conviction, I was walking to the front of the altar. Reverend Seward stood there with arms outstretched, saying it is well. With a public apology to my family during that church service, I felt peace and forgiveness that I can't explain. My parents were well-respected, serving in leadership at Mt. Zion Baptist Church and in the community, yet I was shaming them with my crazy drama. Later, I would hear my dad's words, "It's better you tell your story than someone else."

"Therefore, there is now no condemnation for those who are in Christ Jesus."

(Romans 8:1 NIV)

The road to recovery was a journey paved with rebuilding my trust with others, but more importantly, trusting myself with decisions, choosing to feel the pain of circumstances and not mask the emotions or consequences. I worked on recovering my finances, which were in shambles, and rebuilding and recreating a life based on truths of what I, Kim Denise, bring to the table, knowing that I am enough. The journey of building healthy self-esteem and living life on life's terms took several years. I eventually finished college and purchased my first home, my mansion, for $90,000. The feeling that I had arrived and my life by God's design was on the right track. The feeling of pride was indescribable.

"I thank Christ Jesus our Lord, who has given me strength, that he considered me trustworthy, appointing me to his service. Even though I was once a blasphemer and a persecutor and a violent man, I was shown mercy because I acted in ignorance and unbelief. The grace of our Lord was poured out on me abundantly, along with the faith and love that are in Christ Jesus. Here is a trustworthy saying that deserves full acceptance:

Christ Jesus came into the world to
save sinners—of whom I am the worst.
(1 Timothy 1:12-15 NIV)

Like Paul, I am reminded that my mistakes do not stop me from moving forward with God.

My church roots were going deeper and so was my commitment to God's process and His conviction that my life was becoming what He would say is "well done." That's what I yearned for and that is what has motivated me when storms of life came.

One Wednesday night, during Bible service with Bishop Bolin at Trinity Chapel, he called me out of the congregation, mid-sermon, and asked me to give my testimony on recovery and acknowledge that I am no longer that person.

"Old things have passed away," he said, and I had a new name in Christ to proudly declare and walk with my head held high moving forward. That service opened the door of opportunity for me to launch Celebrate Recovery Small Group, which opened its doors at the local prison for a once-a-week recovery meeting. I still have the prison ID badge that I keep as a reminder of God's grace. God takes our mess, and it becomes the message of the Gospel that will draw others unto Him.

War for your purpose and your destiny. I've learned that people who reject themselves only see their flaws, not the beauty God created in them. Perfect love casts out all fear which means I can have total trust in God and God's process and processing of me. Whatever touches my life, I must believe I can stand up to it.

"And hope does not put us to shame, because God's love has been poured out into our hearts through the Holy Spirit, who has been given to us."

(Romans 5:5 NIV)

God wants the glory out of my walk and testimony. These Scriptures are powerful reminders of His Promise:

"She gave birth to a son, a male child, who "will rule all the nations with an iron scepter." And her child was snatched up to God and to his throne."

(Revelation 12:5 NIV)

"Being confident of this, that he who began a good work in you will carry it on to completion until the day of Christ Jesus."

(Philippians 1:6 NIV)

"To all in Rome who are loved by God and called to be his holy people: Grace and peace to you from God our Father and from the Lord Jesus Christ."

(Romans 1:7 NIV)

"Do not conform to the pattern of this world, but be transformed by the renewing of your mind. Then you will be able to test and approve what God's will is—his good, pleasing and perfect will."

(Romans 12:2 NIV)

"Therefore, if anyone is in Christ, the new creation has come: The old has gone, the new is here!"

(2 Corinthians 5:17 NIV)

Unbr8kable Thoughts:

Self-esteem is developed in three ways—what others say about you, remembering that hurt people hurt others, and what God says about you. List the positive messages of God's Word about you.

_____

_____

_____

_____

_____

Why was it so important for others to approve of me before I embraced the real me?

_____

_____

_____

_____

_____

Who or what do you turn to when you're out of options?

_____

_____

_____

_____

_____

What is the Holy Spirit saying at this moment?

_____

_____

_____

_____

_____

What thing are you standing in faith, believing in God for today?

_____

_____

_____

_____

_____

Do not lay your life down to the devil. Surrender your will to God. He will set you free. Write your surrender statement.

_____

_____

_____

_____

_____

What are the names you have been answering to?

_____

_____

_____

_____

_____

A moment of truth and personal reflection asks the question, "What am I standing on to withstand whatever battle comes my way?"

_____

_____

_____

_____

_____

Damita Wynn

The Pursuit of Happiness

Damita Wynn

It was not simple.

It was not easy.

It was a process.

You see, people always look at the surface yet never know how a diamond is created—the pressure, the time, and the energy. Happiness does not come overnight, and it is shaped by many experiences. Yes, happiness, the diamond of emotions and state of being.

The year 1967 birthed a lump of coal that would be tried by fire. It started rough around the edges because the environment it was birthed into was rough, dark, sad, drab, and dreary. Well into year four, the lump of coal was slowly shedding layers it had been born with, shedding by encounters with others. Preschool was rocked with rejection and shrinking. This behavior continued through kindergarten and elementary school.

It was easy to fit in with the gems. They were rough around the edges and the lump of coal was born into a house of gems. Sometime around the fifth grade, the coal was labeled "average-looking." She had no idea what that meant and did not care. You see, she was evolving into her own. She hung with the gems, fought with the gems, and mimicked a lot of the gems' behaviors. She ran the streets and learned how to use weapons to defend herself, yet she always knew there was a soft side. By middle school, she had shed so much that there was a light that started to beam from her and bounce off her. But she did not want to be a light. She was happy in the dark, in the shadows behind the clouds.

Life continued and the light coming from the coal grew brighter. As the light grew brighter, she covered and hid the light, never wanting anyone to see her light. She began writing and expressing her feelings through poetry. She wrote:

I am not the same.

I do not feel the same.

I tend to hide, yet it is not from shame.

Why are they looking as if I am trying to take what they are presenting when I know that it is fake?

Can I just be who I was created to be without everyone looking and trying to judge me?

When she was around 11 years old, she looked in the mirror and turned to see what others saw. The fact remained that she was thrust into being a caregiver while trying to discover herself. She did not mind though. She loved her family, and it allowed her to be the focus of attention. She did not have to compete with her brothers or little sister. It was just her and her grandmother. They spent days and nights laughing, watching great movies, and eating ice cream or Snickers at midnight. In those moments, she did not realize it was caregiving. She thought she was keeping her grandmother from living alone.

Fast forward to her freshmen year of high school. She met her high school sweetheart. He was two years older. They dated throughout high school. He graduated and went into the military. He would write and send letters through her best friend because her parents told her that he was too old. She made the best of her high school years as editor of the school newspaper and a member of the yearbook staff. She was on the winter and spring dance teams. But again, through these years, she experienced rejection. Her teachers and peers loved her but there was something different about her that people constantly rejected.

Her teachers and peers encouraged her to try out for the captain position and class officer. Politics was not her thing and still is not, so being a class officer was not it. She tried out for dance team captain and nailed the tryouts with her routine, so much so that before the official announcement, it was all over the school how she would be captain. The results were posted, and not only was she not selected as captain, but she was not selected as an officer, either.

Always picking herself up by her bootstraps, she went on to be President of the Black Student Organization where she began coming out of her shy shell. This thrust her into being out front and speaking on behalf of Black students. Senior year came, and it was time to think about college. As a hopeful mass media communication major, she chose Howard University. Yes, an HBCU. She was awarded a scholarship from a small college in Indiana to study journalism, but times were still strange to Black folks.

She was accepted into Howard; however, her parents had other plans—local plans. This took the wind out of her sail. After high school, she went to work. College was still an option, but her energy was failing. Finally, her parents agreed to the local university because her cousin had been selected, so surely, she should go there, too. She signed up for classes but never attended.

Winter came and she was tired of being treated like a kid, so she decided to live with her high school sweetheart and start a life. Two months after being there, he was shipped off to Germany for three months. Left alone in Alexandria, Virginia, she did what she could; however, during his time away, she discovered two life-changing things. One, she was pregnant, and two, the most devastating news, he had not been truthful with her. He was married.

Alone and not knowing what to do, she called an older cousin in DC who began helping her get her life together. When he returned from Germany, he returned with his wife. She was numb at that point and emotionless.

"I'm pregnant," she said.

He was excited.

"And I'm leaving," she said.

The look on his face said it all. She went outside to wait for her cousin to pick her up, and his wife came outside and began to beg her to stay. "He loves you!" the wife said.

Without missing a beat, she responded, "Yet he is married to you."

She left there and never looked back. Her father flew her back to Ohio, and she went on with her life.

Upon returning, she met a young man who accepted her pregnancy. She enrolled in the HBCU close to home and began her college career studying business and journalism. She and the young man eventually got married and had two more children, yet the relationship was full of abuse, rejection, and toxicity.

Finally, after years of abuse, infidelity, and rejection, she was forced to leave the marriage. It was during the divorce process that she took hold of her life and tapped into who she was. She had always been "the pretty one," yet she hated that no one ever really wanted to get to know her. They simply saw her but never knew her. During this period, she focused on herself and her children, understanding who she was and realizing she had spent all her life pleasing everyone except herself. She had conformed to who everyone else wanted her to be and shrank herself to accommodate others' insecurities, hating that her appearance always brought rejection and disdain.

It was not until she felt like she had hit rock bottom and had to move in with her parents with two teenage daughters that she peeled off the cape of rejection and began to walk in her truth to be confident and unapologetic. She no longer allowed others' rejection to shape her life or her thoughts.

She soon met the man of her dreams. He spoke life into her. He saw her heart. While at first, she was not interested, God softened her heart to receive true love and adoration. And when he proposed to her on Christmas Eve of 2011, she said yes.

This lump of coal was allowing her light to shine and for others to see her inner beauty. Several years passed and she was introduced to an organization. She was presented with the opportunity to pledge a Christian sorority. Completing the process, she was named "DeVoted."

How fitting.

How appropriate.

This diamond has been tried in the fire in every conceivable way. She had been through hell and high water. She had been loved, hated, accepted, and rejected, and yet now she sits confidently on who she is, secure in who God has created her to be, unapologetic about her character and integrity, unmoved and unbothered about who does not like her, and blessed with family and friends. Some love her still, others do not. Some have exercised the freedom of getting to know her and others have not. Years ago, that rejection would have caused her to spend energy on situations beyond her control. Today, she is grateful for her scares and the hurt and pain she went through because each experience has contributed to her becoming. Today, she is free from the sting of the opinions of others:

I look back at how life began, how the pathway twisted and turned, how people, places, things, and words caused my heart to burn.

Who can complain when it was all meant to shape me, to lead me to learn to love who God has designed me to be?

There is no peace like the peace of God,

And there is love and happiness in being odd.

Hold your shoulders back and strut your stuff.

You are God's original design.

You are both soft and rough.

She has reached happiness because she has learned that she has been fearfully and wonderfully made by the Master. She is exactly who He called her to be. Humility, dignity, and honor are hers. She is Damita DeVoted Wynn.

Nyree Fray

Pieces of Me
Turning My Baggage into Luggage

Nyree Dawn Fray

I never imagined being in a situation where divorce would be an option and certainly not at the age of 40. I never had a plan B, and I did not plan on being a statistic, not me. Yet here I am. Why me, oh Lord? I went through a battle of questioning what I knew the Holy Spirit told me to do to "set us all free." I knew the situation was dysfunctional and toxic, so when I was awakened from deep sleep to enter the walk-in closet of the master bedroom to pray in the Spirit, I could not deny the voice of God and what I was commanded to do. But how and why did we get here?

I grew up as the middle child, the only girl, and later found out during phase two (post-divorce) that I was a rainbow baby. This concept seemed odd because I never really knew my position within my nuclear family except for the fact that children were seen and not heard. This concept never really made sense, but I had sense enough to know never to say that aloud. As the only girl, I was overly protected, but the nurturing (emotional nurturing, at least) was sorely lacking. My parents gave what they were given which was a strong work ethic that provided a level of stability they were proud to impart. After all, status mattered. My mother was a well-educated registered nurse, and my father was a Vietnam veteran and federal government employee. Both my parents were from Jamaica and were proud of the legacy they created in America. However, this did not come without a price.

Childhood pains were never discussed but were real, felt but unseen. We never talked about it. My mother loved the Lord. Thankfully, she created a space for religion. I remember my water baptism and knowing there was an external force within me that was greater than me and one whom with I would develop a personal relationship. Eventually, the elephant in the room grew between my parents and their marriage abruptly ended in 2006 after 42 years of marriage.

I did not easily or immediately obey the spoken Word. Quite honestly, I did not know how or where to start. So, I began to try to "fix" my marriage. As a counselor, I suggested resources, including individual and family counseling. I figured this could be a midlife crisis. I had been so used to taking care of everything and everyone so this was just more of that, and in due time, I figured the dust would settle and he would begin to feel our love again.

Over two years had gone by, and the level of dysfunction grew unbearably. We had gotten to a place of no trust, deception, rejection, anger, and resentment. I had no choice but to accept the truth which was that the marriage was over. The hurt and pain outweighed the love and honesty and the "in love" had died, too.

I remembered the night I sat in bed, alone, and had a vision of my children looking at me in bed, lifeless, and talking to me, trying to get me to communicate with them, but I was stuck. I immediately came out of the daze and back to reality and said I cannot afford to check out because they would have two emotionally, unhealthy parents, and that was not an option. Before that, I had taken 13 prescription anxiety pills to numb the emotional pain. I was devastated to my core that my marriage was over, and I could not deny it. I was grieving the pain from accepting that my marriage was ending. I accepted the message from God that for all of us to live sustainable, quality, healthy lives, I had to leave my marriage.

I executed what would be my third and final decision to remove my children and me from our family home. This home was specifically built in 2007 as our dream home. This home was supposed to represent stability and longevity for our children as we had several moves before relocating to Covington, Georgia. This home was now filled with an opposing spirit to God and threatened the foundation of our family, marriage, faithfulness, trust, unity, respect, and honor. This home was devalued with new ownership by August 2015.

I no longer recognized the person with whom I shared vows. Our union was officially dissolved by October 2016. I spent the first year of our separation relocating to Ohio with our two children and the family bulldog. I had written a proposal to my employer, requesting 100% remote working with the caveat of flying back to Georgia, quarterly, at my expense. After all, my personal life created this scenario. I did not have a plan B, so I was simply going through the motions of life. Emotional pain is devastating, and I did not fully understand the magnitude of the pain my children and I were experiencing. I did not realize that with obedience comes complete sacrifice and submission. Yet, the next five-year journey would reveal how we ended up in this place.

I was 21 years old when I took my vows. I was certain I would be married until death do us part. I never considered myself the dating type, and I had watched my mother be the submissive wife that the Bible mentions. I had always felt wifely, and I knew I wanted to have children one day, so marriage made sense. When my husband pursued me, I did not have any reason to doubt his love for me and vice versa. I was happy to be away from my controlling parents and ready to make real-life decisions. Initially, they seemed supportive, but like clockwork, the tables turned, and we ended up eloping when my father threatened to disown me if I "shacked up."

Remember, we had an image to maintain.

Speaking of which, we committed to a "real" wedding for family and friends on our first wedding anniversary. Looking back, this represents one of many pivotal moments of us allowing my family to be intrusive. There was always an overarching feeling of resorting to being a child any time my parents had an opinion because "children are seen and not heard." I disagreed but it was a behavior I learned and struggled to balance, even as a young, married, independent adult.

There were many years of growing pains and trying to find our paths as a young couple, becoming parents within three years, his mother's cancer diagnosis, and her death. Her death was another pivotal memory because I can pinpoint that time as a period when his depression, childhood unforgiveness, and resentment toward my family presented themselves. I did as my mother did by instilling church and a love for God in our household from the start. We had both grown up in the church with differing outcomes (experiences). I willfully attended, and it did not feel forced on as if it was a chore. Over time, attending church as a family became less and less a priority but I continued to involve my children and myself. God was the ultimate foundation of who I was, and I honored that relationship as best I knew.

Divorce was inevitable. I did not have a plan B because I was living it. Plan A is now. Plan A is God's plan. The desires of my heart are fulfilled. The testimony must be shared. The message is to submit to the Will of God. If we chose to exercise our free will instead of His Will, we delay. Delayed obedience is disobedience. God knows the desires of our hearts because He planted them from the time of conception. I am a rainbow baby with a Rhema word. My testimony is real, and God saved my eternal life.

Six years later, I have completed my root work which includes inner healing ministry, mental health counseling, the fruition of prophetic words spoken into my life, utilizing my gifting as an intercessor, and pledging a Christian sorority to share my testimony in hopes to offer hope. I had to go through the process of learning how to pray and fast to live through the near-death experience of my father, the death of a partner, the death of friends to illnesses, medical surgery, and the traumatic experiences of my children as a result of the divorce, being obedient to three specific encounters with the Holy Spirit:

1. Leave to save our lives.

2. Do not marry the false prophet.

3. Yes to Kenneth.

In hindsight, I understand that I had to experience all of the trials and tribulations to be reminded that God is the key priority. Prayer is a weapon, and my desire was not just to get married to have a husband. I desired a covenant spouse who prayed for me as much as I prayed for him in unity for the work of Christ to honor the Word of God in our relationship. God had to prepare me to be ready to accept this mantle and to show I would stay on the wall if it were His Will.

Korean V. Peoples

Becoming "In-Power"
in the Midst of Grief

Korean V. Peoples

Korean means inhabiting; a beautiful maiden.
In Latin, it means spear. In-power means expression of the
situation; expression of movement.

I come from a long line of strong women. I have heard stories
of my Madea (great-grandmother), my grandmother's mother. But
I tell you, witnessing the strength of my grandmother, Delores
"Julie" Brown-Mayfield, was the start of my journey. She seemed
to handle each obstacle with ease. Then came my mom. I watched
her work and take care of four daughters, keep us fed, clothed, and
in extracurricular activities while allowing us to be ourselves,
along with her taking care of her husband. I also watched her
overcome obstacles and beat many odds. Watching these great

women made me feel as if life was handled as easy as it all seemed, then, for sure, I inherited that strength, too.

I lost my sister in 1988, one of my first strength tests. I am not sure where the strength came from, but it had to be God. Not only was I the last person to talk to my sister, but I helped prepare her for burial. I did her hair and make-up, helped dress her, and spoke and sang at her funeral. The Lord was my driver at that time.

I made it to the other side of my sister's death, by the grace and mercy of God. The next year, I was married, and life was grand. I had two beautiful children, but the marriage began to fail fast. This was the first time in my life that every ounce of my strength had vanished. The magnitude of hurt I felt sent me into a downward spiral of depression, insecurity, self-doubt, and weakness. I swore I would not date for five years, but God had a different plan for my life.

Dedicated to Widows

I met and married the most magnificent man. He was my fairytale, a dream come true. He treated me like a queen. When you saw one of us, you knew the other was not far away. We worked well together. I learned through the love he gave that I deserved it. My depression and insecurity were gone, and my strength was back.

When life is grand, you are all smiles, but when life is happening and out of control in a way you never planned or imagined, you often wonder what to do. I have always been a God-fearing, powerhouse woman, at least in my eyes. If you thought a person was the epitome of strength, that also would be me. But my entire life changed on May 4, 2013. That powerhouse pillar of strength went from 1,000 to zero. The strength I managed to build over the last 15 years had vanished in a blink of an eye. I was back to being that scared little girl bullied in first grade and that young woman mistreated in her first marriage. All the bravery I thought I had was gone.

How would I deal with this permanent change in my life, a change that sent my heart plummeting to my feet, knocked the air out of my lungs, and blew every strand of hair on my head back? How would I get my strength back, let alone live a life of normalcy?

God had taken back the man He sent me—no warning, just gone. In fact, I thought it should have been me. After all, I was the one in the hospital that day.

A journey of grief is worse than a horror movie. At least there are only fear and anxiety while watching the movie, but with grief, there is so much more: a range of emotions, numbness, weakness, abandonment, shock, depression, hazards to your health, mourning, and anger. That is a lot to contend with if you do not go insane.

A Temporary Mental Breakdown

It does not matter how many people are around you because you don't really see them anyway. Everything is a blur. And so it began, step one: Acknowledgement. I had to acknowledge the reality that my husband had passed away. He was no longer breathing, and his heart was no longer beating. He was gone.

Step two: Preparations to bury my husband.

"Oh my gosh. I am burying my husband," I continually thought in horror.

In my case, I had to sign for him to be released from the coroner's office, drive at least one hour to the mortuary, pick out clothes and programs, and write an obituary. I did it all.

Step three: The viewing. I remember his cold and lifeless body and wanting this to be a bad dream or a horror movie because the movie would have ended, and he would still be here. Sadly, his death was not a bad dream or a movie.

Step four: The funeral. It was a blur.

Step five: The burial/repass. This was my final goodbye, my breaking point, and the last time I could see his earthly body. My strength was gone again. The repass was another blur for my shattered heart.

Of course, when it's over, you get a few calls and visits, but it is easier to stay in bed and cry. I am grateful to my children, family, and two special friends. Had it not been for them, I could have easily checked out mentally.

So, here we are. The fog is starting to lift, and by the time I started emerging from my dark sad place, years had passed. I had been walking, talking, bathing, and working, but I was not present. I found out how going through the motions was quite easy. More grief came as I lost my grandmother and a cousin. Grief was coming left and right.

Well, there is one sure thing I can tell you about coming out of grief. Well, two things. First: Take it one step at a time. Actually, one step at a time will be all you can take because your equilibrium will be off. You will almost want to tiptoe. Secondly, there is no time limit. Please do not try to rush grief. You really can't because grief has a way of maintaining its presence, simply because of the absence of your loved one.

Here I am, eight years later. Lord knows I have tried to be present. When you are in the midst of grief, you do and say all sorts of things, things you remember and things you want to forget, including people, places, and things.

Although I felt like I was in the middle of the ocean without a life vest, I found that God was there all along. I had to go through the grieving process and trust in God to help me get up again. I am back, and not only am I back, but I am strong.

I am trusting and leaning on God like never before. Going through this started my spiritual maturity, and I am grateful. God saw fit for me to endure so that I could understand that His joy comes in the morning. I learned that you must be twisted, pulled, poked, examined, and polished like a diamond.

God saw my heart. He gave me the love of a grandson, whom I call "Heartbeat," and He helped me through the storm. Watching the Lord mold this awesome, God-fearing, loving child was the best. I am grateful beyond measure.

God has a way with divine intervention. He is truly amazing. When I mention divine intervention, I am referring to how God purposely moves people into places and performs miracles.

I trusted God, and He worked on me from the inside out. He transformed me, but most of all, He loves me with my flaws, especially in my brokenness. I can rejoice in the good times with my husband, Reuben Lindale Peoples, my forever guardian angel. He is smiling that awesome smile because I am finally moving forward and taking the love we had for each other to another level by telling my testimony of how God has healed me. I am caring for and counseling widows like myself and helping many people through their grief. This journey of *Becoming "In-Power" in the Midst of Grief* has not been easy, but by the grace of God, I made it.

Thank you to my wonderful husband. I love you forever. Rest in peace. Thank you to my children, family, friends, and TAU for loving God and His Word and loving me!

I Am In-Powered to Empower!

Luke 10:19-20 reminds us:

I have given you authority to trample on snakes and scorpions and to overcome all the power of the enemy; nothing will harm you. However, do not rejoice that the spirits submit to you, but rejoice that your names are written in heaven (NIV).

If you are dealing with grief and need to find your way to the other side, contact me on Facebook, *Korean Peoples,* or *Women's Think Tank,* or on Instagram. Women's Think Tank, Inc. is a non-profit organization that focuses on widows and how to prepare them to restore and rejuvenate themselves through prayer, seminars, and other recreational outings. Korean is also the owner of Bling and Blessing Boutique, Ama's Luv, and Ama's Luv in the Kitchen. Coming in the near future: *How to Keep Going When You Lose Your Significant Other and "How to Get Your Happiness Out of Lay-Away.*

Raychelle Lee

Becoming Her

Building Noble Character

Raychelle Lee

"A wife of noble character who can find?
She is worth far more than rubies."

(Proverbs 31:10 NIV)

Every life has a turning point, a moment when experiences and life lessons change everything.

For me, that moment came when I decided to follow the wisdom of God versus the ways of the world. The idea of being a wise woman having good experiences, knowledge, good judgment, and pleasing in the eyesight of the Lord had become one of the greatest desires for my life.

After a series of bad decisions, causing great amounts of heartache, grief, and money, I knew I had to make drastic changes, not only for me but for my two innocent daughters depending on me.

I got pregnant with my first child when I was 26 years old by my boyfriend who had been my best friend since the eighth grade. When I became pregnant, our relationship fell apart, and we had gone our separate ways by my sixth month of pregnancy. I was sad but the excitement of the baby kept me going.

After my daughter was born, I returned to work, and that is where I met my first husband. We dated for one year before getting married. It was a rocky year, and it was evident we should not have gotten married. After two and half years of being in a toxic marriage, I found myself pregnant with my second child. Infidelity and lack of trust from both of us landed us in divorce court by the time my daughter was three months old.

I found myself divorced with two children and two different fathers. I was hurt, ashamed, and embarrassed. In the apostolic faith, having children out of wedlock and being divorced was frowned upon, and I was told I could never marry again, or I would be considered an adulterer and my second marriage would not be recognized in the church. I believed my life was doomed until I returned to church and began my journey of learning and becoming a Proverbs 31 woman.

My journey began after the divorce with my first husband and the painful custody battle with my first child's father. I had to repent for my sins and rededicate my life to the Lord. Second, I began attending church regularly and reading my Word daily. I, as well as others, began to see changes in my life. Thirdly, I knew I wanted to remarry so I begin to talk to, watch, and ask questions to wives I esteemed to be virtuous women about how to be a good, Godly wife. Lastly, I began to change my ways like cursing, fornicating, drinking, and any other sins I was committing. This was my prayer:

Heavenly Father, I am humbly coming before You asking for Your guidance during this journey to become the woman You created me to be when I was in my mother's womb. Remove anything in me preventing me from being that "good thing" for my husband or future husband, so that he may obtain favor from You. Teach me what "noble character" means in Your eyes and not the world's perspective so that I may live accordingly. Lord, encourage and empower me to draw closer to You as I begin to learn more about myself. Help me to accept, love, and see myself as You see me—"Worth far more than rubies." As I study the Scriptures, please help me to have a full understanding of Your Word and apply it to my life daily. Also, teach and guide me to the places to be found by (insert what you are waiting for – career opportunities, job, husband, etc).

So, Lord, as I take this journey to build noble character and find the woman within that You created me to be, I trust that You will never leave nor forsake me. Amen.

A Proverbs 31 woman is not just a married woman with children. Your marital or parental status does not qualify you; your character and relationship with God do. Preparing to become a virtuous woman meant I had to work diligently to live a life that glorifies, honors, and draws me closer to God first. Regardless of my marital and parental status, preparing to become a woman of noble character ranked in priority daily.

The virtuous woman became an amazing woman because she knew and feared God. She knew who she was and what she wanted out of life. Her goal was simply to please God. When I became obedient to the Word of God, everyone around me was pleased or they left. Do not allow distractions to steer you from the direction God is leading you. If someone leaves or you lose something, God will keep you at perfect peace and will restore you tenfold. Although trials and tribulations will come, standing and being focused on the Word of God will keep you and block unnecessary troubles that arise from disobedience.

Who can find? Meaning she is not easy to find. Her presence is not easily accessed by just anyone. She is a hidden gem, not easy to discover. This type of woman is selective of where she goes. She seeks God's direction and wisdom in every area of her life. She is not as the world would call "thirsty."

A virtuous woman does not hang out in places or with people that do not enhance her life or encourage her to fulfill her God-given purpose. She is engulfed in pleasing God, so unless you are a man or woman after God's heart, you will miss her.

Why?

Because she is a priceless hidden gem. She is worth far more than rubies. She knows her worth, adds value to her family, and knows that priceless gems are not easily accessible.

She is held in high regard by God, her husband, children, friends, family, and all those wise enough to know her worth. When something is valuable, it is not handled like everything or everybody. It is not treated as something or someone common. For instance, let's say a person craves a Godiva chocolate bar at two in the morning. First of all, Godiva is not sold everywhere, and it is priced much higher than the average candy bar. A person would have to wait until reasonable hours and know exactly which stores sell them. A person would have to put effort into purchasing a Godiva chocolate bar. Many times, the craving is out of selfishness, greed, or undisciplined habits, so they would settle for less. If the person truly wants a Godiva chocolate bar, they will put forth the effort to obtain one, which means they will more than likely appreciate the taste and purchase additional bars for a later time because they are not easy to obtain.

On the other hand, M&Ms are everywhere and can be purchased at any time, even on a whim. There is no effort in finding them and people usually do not appreciate them because it takes no effort or much thought. More importantly, everyone has access because their value is very cheap.

Amedei Porcelana is dark chocolate made by the Amedei chocolatier of Tuscany, Italy. In the United States, a 1.8-ounce bar sells for $18.99 or $90 per pound.

So, who can find this expensive chocolate?

Those that can afford it and those in the exclusive class who would even know it exists.

That's how I want to be—so rare, hidden, and expensive that the average person can't afford to find me or know I exist unless they are engulfed in the presence of the Lord.

From one virtuous woman to the next, I want you to search within yourself and go back to the very beginning when God gave you the knowledge of the greatness on the inside of you, and call forth those things that you know into your now and any place of weakness. I want you to present those places to God and be aware of how they have affected your past and how they affect you now and take every day to perfect that place. If there are any days you may fall short of who you want to become, get back up and get that thing right within yourself, with God, and with people. Being intentional about your growth is mandatory because if we give excuses for places of weakness, that will always remain who we are, and virtuosity will never reside, but foolishness will remain.

The Bible is never short of any examples of strength, whether male or female. The Word remains the same, and we can draw from these biblical principles and lessons. David was a prime example and a great one for everybody to see strengths and weaknesses. We can take a lifetime to study who He is and still obtain much more.

Most of us can attest that there has been one person in our life over the years that has been a natural example of virtuousness. So, let's call these people to our remembrance. Let us study their lives and what we know about them to mentally feed ourselves examples of those that have gone before us to tell our brains it is possible to be stronger than what we are or to be better than anything we have ever seen.

Daily Affirmation
(Recite while looking at yourself in a mirror):
I AM fearfully and wonderfully made and hidden in the presence of the Lord.
I AM virtuous.

Stacie Hayes

One Who Shall Rise Again

Stacie Hayes

Writing the vision about me so I can right the vision around me speaks to the One who shall rise again. How do you rise when you do not know you should be standing? How do you rise when you do not recognize your value? How do you rise when you do not know you are bent over and stepped on and over? How?

I had to recognize that I am a L.A.D.Y. This revelation did not happen overnight nor at an early age, but it has and continues to be in me. When I understood what being is not and embraced what God told me a L.A.D.Y. should be, He said to me:

Lead with purpose.

Always walk with your head held high.

Develop like a diamond.

Your actions will keep you a lady.

I understood everything except developing like a diamond. God explained to me that I must recognize I am rare like diamonds. I needed to understand my worth. I needed to understand the four Cs of a diamond: cut, carat, color, and clarity. He showed me that I must first cut my personal "niche" in the earth that will positively affect the Kingdom. Secondly, in a diamond, the carat carries weight, so I am to understand and know my worth. Next, I need to see and recognize the color of my beautiful reflection, not only for me to see in the mirror, but also for others. Finally, I must have the clarity of who God has made me be for self and others to see. He allowed me to remember that diamonds form on the deep and dark surfaces of the Earth. A diamond is the hardest substance on Earth that exists naturally. Developed under pressure, and yet when polished, it shines beautifully. It was made clear to me that I do not have a price tag; therefore, I cannot be bought.

In the making of my life, there have been pressures, some from me and some from others. As I think about my journey, I am now fine with this journey of recognizing who I am. It is my story, not to be measured or compared to others. It is my story, validated by God, and that is enough. The Father showed me who I am and whose I am with my birth name of Stacie and my newly given name in the spring of 2021.

One day, as a teenager, I looked in the mirror and said, "Stacie! Stacie! I like my name." It was funny hearing me say it and embracing it in a new light. One might say you have heard your name called many times, so what was different? That time, I heard it with a new ear. I looked up the meaning of my name to learn that it means "one who shall rise again or resurrect." I took it to mean that I would see traits in others and myself to help them or I get to where they or I need to go in life. I never thought I would fall within or need to get up from being stepped on emotionally.

Now reflecting on that moment, I wonder when I stopped hearing who I am as a confident and proud young lady. Was it when I asked my grandmother about something personal, and she accused me of doing something improper as a young college student? Since it was my first time being away from home, I was excited, nervous, and scared at the same time. So, I was not doing anything out of order. That response silenced me from ever asking her anything important to me. I know some would say that should not have stopped me, but just like continual slow drops of water can erode the dirt beneath your feet, so can words when one seeks wisdom, and it is not given no matter how simple. One never realizes how fragile a person can be by just looking at them. Words create worlds, some positive and some negative, so we need to pay attention to what we say. The effects could affect an individual for the good or the bad, so tread lightly.

As an 11 or 12-year-old, I had an experience that has shaped me to this day. One day, a first cousin came to visit from one of the northern states. She was only about 14 or 15 years old. I remember clearly that we were standing in the kitchen, and the television was on with a popular show that had several different characters. This cousin saw one of the characters making a strange noise, and out of the blue, she said, "We're going to make your nickname that sound!"

I am not sure where the courage came from within, but I immediately said, "You will never call me that name," and shut that issue down. The power of words is particularly important to me. I do not know if it started there, but that situation is the reason I do not care for nicknames unless it is a name of endearment or empowerment. Looking back on that situation, not realizing I innocently accepted people as they were without judgment, but because of the situation with my young cousin, a defense mechanism developed that I had no idea existed as an adult today.

The importance of words and tone never occurred to me. As I fast forward several years, not realizing there must have been other times I avoided and kept silent when words spoken to me had slowly crushed me, silence became a defensive mechanism that morphed into me making sure that whatever I did would not be ridiculed or judged. I wanted it to be enough without fault so I would not hear crushing words.

Some might say they did not mean it to be hurtful or that I was just blowing things out of proportion. Some of that might be true, but when you are young and seeking validation from those closest to you, words stick like glue, and you do not even realize it.

The Womb World – Another Defense Mechanism

Although I was in this world, I found myself in a womb in the comforts of my own world. It was easy and safe not to allow anyone to get too close to me, always thinking about what they wanted and what they would say about me. This so-called "womb world" I have coined allowed me to be in control of what I would accept. In this world, I believe I have lost financially, physically, and spiritually in many ways. When one does not trust life's processes, they lose out on what could have been a beautiful return on the experiences.

It left me distrusting others.

I am a work in progress, and I am fine with that.

To help paint the picture, here is another example that sticks with me to this very day. I attended a church that I love. Because of who my mother is, you could never go to church without presenting yourself to God in your best attire. I fondly remember getting my hair washed on Saturday night and having my hair pressed or permed—the dreaded perm (I am forgetting that forever!) We always had cute dresses with matching socks and bows. You get the picture. Well, fast forward to my adult life. This has made me love, love, and one more love, a beautiful dress.

So, one Sunday, I was in the lobby of the church, and another lady my age walked up to me and said, "You'll never be a certain way." (The actual subject matter is not important, but just know it had something to do with my physical look.) What was said threw me for a loop because I thought that person was my friend. This made me avoid her, and then one Sunday, she cornered me in the parking lot to ask why I avoided her. I said, "Because I never know what you might say to me," and I walked off. That was the beginning of me not trusting in a positive way without realizing it. Maturity in our Heavenly Father would have spoken words of encouragement and healing instead of avoiding and running away. Instead of being the one who "resurrects" the beauty in people, I was silenced by what others said to me.

My New Birth Name, Born March 27, 2021

John 15:1-3 ASV:

I am the true vine, and my Father is the husbandman. Every branch in me that beareth not fruit, he taketh it away: and every branch that bearth fruit, he cleanseth it, that it may bear more fruit. Already ye are clean because of the word which I have spoken unto you.

The footnote for this passage states that as a husbandman, you invest in the land you are cultivating. Because of the care taken with the land, there is an expectation for it to produce the good fruit sown. This is an investment our Heavenly Father has sown in us because of His sacrifice on the cross. We are purposed to produce good fruit. Although we cannot control the environment around us, we can control our inner environment. Our inner environment is our mind and soul.

Acceptance from the One Who Made Me

Do you remember when I shared that I loved my name? I still do, but in the spring of 2021, I was given a new name. My new name is "Tru-Vine," and I love this name, too. It speaks to me because this was the last of the seven "I AM" declarations recorded in John's Gospel by Jesus. The research tells me these "I AM" proclamations pointed to His unique divine identity and purpose. My purpose and identity with this new birth name have allowed me to embrace this name because they allow the following:

Trimming of my branches of weaknesses in trusting.
Reaching for the branches of love and peace.
Undoing fixtures within of thinking I am not enough.
Vulnerability to the Master Gardener is painful but necessary.
Inking in what I once wrote with a pencil, ready to erase to not be ridiculed or belittled by harsh words.
Now, but now I know who I am and whose I am.
Excited about the pruning and care from the Master Gardner.

The name "Tru-Vine" has energized me to live more for the Kingdom because it is a continued reminder that I was born for a purpose and on purpose. I know we were not born to be a part of the formula of being just **born** + **existing** equaling **death** (slumbering in B.E.D.), but my purpose tells me that I was born for **being** + **existing** equaling my **destiny** (jumping up and down on the B.E.D.!) So, I embrace my new name birthed on March 27, 2021, so I can fulfill one other area in my God-given destiny. I am still a work in progress. Recognizing that my purpose for being named Tru-Vine is still unfolding, my goal is to make the Father proud so that when I enter Heaven, He will say, "Well done, my good and faithful servant." I was made on purpose and for purpose and that is why I am Tru-Vine.

Cherise Lenore Riley

Destined to Overcome
The Power of Knowing Who You Are

Cherise Lenore Riley

"For I know the plans and thoughts that I have for you,' says the
LORD, 'plans for peace and well-being and not for disaster, to
give you a future and a hope."

(Jeremiah 29:11 Amplified)

The first time I read Jeremiah 29:11, it was as if the words leaped off the page and floated in the air in front of my face, each word burning itself in my brain to become a part of me. It was as if God wanted this Scripture to be written upon the tables of my heart, and at the time, I did not understand why. However, through the years, I would come to understand this message and the power it would hold to help me finally overcome and be free. You see, I was 14 years old when I had this experience and encounter with God when He spoke to me and told me the words of Jeremiah

29:11. Though He assured me of this Scripture's promise, He also told me that things would get worse before they would get better. I was confused because, by the time I had turned 14, I had been through countless traumas. God had a purpose and a plan for my life. It was a plan He formulated before I was born, and because of His purpose and plan for me, another plan was also put into motion. This plan was formed to counteract what God had already spoken and declared. This plan was designed by the enemy, and its purpose was to keep me distracted, angry, and stuck in condemnation so that I would remain blind to my true identity because as long as I didn't know who I truly was and the power of my name, I would never see the path that would lead me back to God's plan.

At two years old, the first blow was sent my way, and by the time I was 14, I had already experienced abandonment, rejection, low self-esteem, abuse, incest, and molestation. I had been called every name in the book, except my actual name, and was told I would never be anything, no one would ever love me or want me, and that I would end up like my biological mother battling drug addiction. I was called ugly and endured physical abuse and torment behind closed doors and was made to believe I deserved everything that had happened to me. The young girl who once had hopes and dreams, goals, and a zest for life had become an empty shell where life no longer seemed to matter and good didn't exist, only illusions. I had become a captive in my mind, and just when I thought things could not get any worse, the bottom fell out. Though

I had already experienced sexual abuse at a very young age, I was brutally raped and beaten when I turned 15, this being the final straw to shatter my self-esteem and destroy, or so I thought, my identity.

On the outside looking in, I had the "charmed life"—a well-known, financially secure family, nice home, nice clothes, vacations, trips, and family get-togethers. The picture looked beautiful to the naked eye but if you looked closer, you would have seen a broken and shattered little girl, struggling to survive, a little girl who had lost her identity and innocence and was on the verge of losing hope. This little girl was me, and I used to imagine how my life would be when I grew up and all the amazing things I would do in the world. However, those imaginations were short-lived because life as I knew it had changed, and this change caused me to crawl within myself and hide. After all, the pain, rejection, and hurt I had endured were unbearable. I allowed the words spoken over me to consume me, and I believed them. I wondered who would or could love me if I was, indeed, all those things.

Even though I smiled on the outside, no one could see the deep pain I carried on the inside. They couldn't see my scars or wounds. I was desensitized to the world. My expectation for good things, a better life, and real love was nonexistent. I only expected bad outcomes because that's all that life had shown me. I didn't understand my purpose of being, and at the time, I began to feel like my encounter and experience with God was only a figment of my imagination, a false glimmer of hope and light that I wished was real, yet trauma and deadly words spoken over me made me believe I had made it all up. I had forgotten the warning I was given in that encounter, that it would get worse before getting better. I felt lost and alone, and I did not trust anyone, nor did their words carry any weight with me; they were empty and fell to the ground. Everyone's motives were questioned and under scrutiny, because let's face it, anything that appeared to be good had a price tag attached to it, and I had nothing left to give. I had more walls up than the walls of Jericho, and I refused to allow them to be knocked down. I refused to show people the real me, but I had no clue who that was anymore. I was lost, and I did not recognize myself nor did I know my purpose any longer. I felt that suicide was my only option, and I had tried to take my life three times by the time I turned 20.

And we know [with great confidence] that God [who is deeply concerned about us] causes all things to work together [as a plan] for good for those who love God, to those who are called according to His plan and purpose. For those whom He foreknew [and loved and chose beforehand], He also predestined to be conformed to the image of His Son [and ultimately share in His complete sanctification], so that He would be the firstborn [the most beloved and honored] among many believers. And those whom He predestined, He also called; and those whom He called, He also justified [declared free of the guilt of sin]; and those whom He justified, He also glorified [raising them to a heavenly dignity] (Romans 8:28-30 Amplified).

Little did I know, things were about to change. There was a light at the end of the tunnel that began to peek through, and I would slowly begin to climb out of my hole, cautiously lowering some of my walls, even though there were still attacks waiting. This time, God would intervene in a way I hadn't expected. See, I thought God had left me after my encounter at 14, when, in fact, I would soon realize that He was always there. It was because of His strength, grace, and mercy protecting me and covering me that had been keeping me during the worst seasons of my life, even when I tried to give up. God knew that the purpose He had created me for was greater than the pain I had endured. At that moment, my journey began on the path toward awakening to who I was created and purposed to be and the power behind the identity of Cherise Lenore. I was beginning a new journey, and this time, I was on the right path. I soon discovered that the power of my name was always at work inside of me, and even though I could not see it at the time, every time it was spoken, the power behind it was being spoken and declared over my life.

The meaning and etymology of Cherise (in Greek and Hebrew) is much beloved, a favorite, graceful, worthy important person, honorable, high price, highly valued, close to the heart, and present in mind.

Che: God will increase.

Rise: Move from a lower place to a higher place; upward movement; an increase in amount and size.

Lenore (in Greek): Light; something that makes vision possible; a source of illumination.

Blessed [fortunate, prosperous, and favored by God] is the man who does not walk in the counsel of the wicked] following their advice and example], nor stand in the path of sinners, nor sit [down to rest] in the seat of scoffers [ridiculers]. But his delight is in the law of the Lord, and on His law [His precepts and teachings] he [habitually] meditates day and night. And he will be like a tree firmly planted [and fed] by streams of water, which yields its fruit in its season; its leaf does not wither; and in whatever he does, he prospers [and comes to maturity] (Psalm 1:1-3 Amplified).

There is an undeniable power that comes with knowing exactly who you are—not just the "who" you were named by your parents, the degree you stand behind, being a mother, wife, husband, or any other title you have picked up along the way, but the real you. There is an undeniable power that comes with knowing the you that God created, ordained, predestined to be, and whose purpose is being birthed out of the pain, hard times, disappointments, rejection, abandonment, anger, and fear along with everything else that has been thrown your way. Our identity is just like a root of a tree; it's that thing buried deep underground. Depending on how it's cultivated will determine how it grows and what it produces. Your life and path become the branches, leaves, and fruit of that tree that has grown because of the roots and soil. Sometimes, the soil gets contaminated, causing the branches to wither and the tree to produce rotten fruit or not produce at all. Some branches get weak and fall away, and depending on the weather and season, all the leaves may disappear. But our identity, just like a tree, has cycles.

What do I mean by that?

I'm glad you asked.

Trees produce based on the season and environment. Likewise, our lives produce, or change, based on the season, environment, and chapter. Our environment speaks of the soil we are using to fortify and feed our roots. If we are feeding it soil laced in bitterness and pain from our past or current experiences, then what we produce will be tainted because we have allowed our identity to be fed by the lies and illusions of our pain. If we feed it soil laced in the promises, wisdom, and knowledge of God and who God created you to be, and if we meditate on it day and night, speaking life to those things that are not as though they were, then the soil will become rich and moist, causing our roots (identity) to be strengthened, sending the signal to our branches to produce leaves so that good fruit will begin to grow on our trees.

Despite the first half of my life and the constant blows I endured, my doubt of God and His plan for my life, my identity (root) was already established and formed. Our fight in life is not to create our identity because God has already done that. Our fight is to be awakened to our true identity, and once we are awakened, we must keep it built up and fortified, not by dwelling on the past and the pain, but by habitually meditating on God's Word concerning us.

It's in this posture that I began to see clearly. When I took my eyes off what I had been through, who hurt me, who left me, who disappointed me, who broke me, and the damage I caused (yes, some of our pain is self-inflicted), I was able to enter into a place of inner healing and deliverance so that I could be fed properly by the Holy Spirit to be strengthened while my mind was renewing, my heart was mending, and my wounds were being sealed. The more I leaned into God, the more He opened my eyes and allowed me to see and embrace who I was and the power that came with it. Revelation 12:10-11 reads:

Then I heard a loud voice in heaven, saying, "Now the salvation, and the power, and the kingdom (dominion, reign) of our God, and the authority of His Christ have come; for the accuser of our [believing] brothers and sisters has been thrown down [at last], he who accuses them and keeps bringing charges [of sinful behavior] against them before our God day and night. And they overcame and conquered him because of the blood of the Lamb and because of the word of their testimony, for they did not love their life and renounce their faith even when faced with death (Amplified Bible).

The thing I love about God is that He wrote the ending of our story before He wrote the beginning. His ending is far better than anything I could imagine for my life. His ending says I win, I overcome, and victory belongs to me. To have the ending God promised requires me to put in some work, but this work, though it may seem too much at times, is nothing compared to the work God has already done on our behalf. I'm not just referring to the final ending of your book or the book of Cherise Lenore. I'm talking to the end of every chapter as well. You see, I went through 20 chapters before I had my "ah-ha" moment, and those chapters were run-ons with no end because I was so engulfed with pain that I couldn't see the purpose until I reached chapter 21. There have been 25 more chapters written since then, and the difference between chapters one through 20 and 21 through 46 is that when I hit 21, I had tapped into my identity. I hadn't mastered it yet, but I also didn't crumble so easily at the first sign of trouble.

Oh, you thought all your troubles would end when you tap into the power of who you are?

Not at all.

They don't end, but they do become easier, and over time, the more you stand firm in your identity, the more you understand your purpose. Some of the tests that come your way will be won before they reach you. Victory comes when you find your freedom to speak freely about your chapters without shame, embarrassment, or condemnation. This is when you tap into the power and authority you were given and the weight of who you are and your purpose on this Earth that causes you to no longer be held captive or paralyzed by trauma. When I stepped in the power of purpose and destiny, I then tapped into my identity and the power of my name. This is when I truly began to understand and tap into the end of my name Che*rise*:

R – Recreating my life and overcoming obstacles by

I – Illuminating God's presence and purpose while

S – Securing my identity to

E – Evolve and transcend into my destiny.

I challenge you to redefine and recreate your identity in Christ. No longer do you have to settle for who the world, your family, or yourself have called you to be. The power of true identity is on the inside of you waiting to be unlocked and discovered.

What's stopping you from opening the door?

What's preventing you from your awakening experience?

There is so much more to your life. God does not have a respecter of person. What He did for me, He is waiting to do for you, too. I dare you to remove the dirt and take another look at the roots of what God created inside of you. What you see will be far greater than the false reality you have been living. I challenge you to change your soil, uproot the seeds you have allowed to be planted, trim your branches, and water your roots and soil with the Word of God. Then, watch the difference in the fruit you produce.

What is your name?

_____

_____

_____

_____

What does it mean?

_____

_____

_____

_____

What has God destined for you to become?

_____

_____

_____

_____

A Tau Lady Anthology Authors

Rev. Michelle L. Dixon, born and raised in Ohio, is a wife, mother, and grandmother who is affectionately called "Mim." A graduate of two HBCUs, Wilberforce University and Payne Theological Seminary, Michelle is an adjunct instructor and Student Success Coach at Wright State University as well as an ordained minister. Those are the roles she occupies, but what she wants people to know and remember most about her is that her identity is a servant of the most high God, called to the community of God's people to serve, teach, counsel, embrace, liberate, and empower, to tell a dying world that a Savior died so that we may live. Michelle joined Tau Alpha Delta Christian Sorority, Inc. in February 2020, and her sorors call her "In-Sightful."

Facebook: @Michelle L. Dixon-MDiv
Instagram: @msshelldixon
Email: mdixon584@gmail.com

Erika Lee, AKA Sistah E, is an author whose work is a classic example of art imitating life. She is a worshiper after God's own heart. She has also been known to make any event memorable as mistress of ceremonies extraordinaire. She gives her readers an in-depth look into the lives of her characters as she brings them to life, inspired by her life experiences, her two young adult sons, and her work as a certified life consultant. As the Founder of Dreamgirl Empowerment Group, Sistah E seeks to help women find and fulfill their God-given purpose. Erika joined Tau Alpha Delta Christian Sorority, Inc. in April 2017, and her sorors call her "Bless2B."

Facebook: @ErikaSupermamaLee
Instagram: @supermamalee_
Email: SistaE123@gmail.com
Website: www.SistaE.chat

Kim Arrington has a Bachelor of Science in criminal justice from Mercer University, is a licensed and ordained minister, graduate of Antioch Bible College, licensed mortgage professional, and diversity and community engagement director. Her true passion for helping others collides within the financial services industry. She educates, equips, and empowers individuals, focusing on budgeting, disciplines, and credit awareness as the key foundational pieces toward increasing the purchasing power in the Black community. She is a wife and mother of three sons. In her leisure time, Kim enjoys puzzles, reading, and yoga. Kim joined Tau Alpha Delta Christian Sorority, Inc. in May 2015, and her sorors call her "Unbr8kable."

Facebook: @kim.arrington.52
Website: bit.ly/kimarrington

Damita L. Wynn is a native of Ohio. She is also a wife, mother, and grandmother. Walking in her passion to encourage and empower women of all ages while equipping them to build their confidence in Christ to avoid the pitfalls of life was the birthing ground for her organization H.E.R. L.I.P.S. Damita's boldness and compassion have opened the door for her as a sought-out speaker and host of conferences, retreats, and workshops. Damita is also the CEO of D'Elegance Event Planning. Damita joined Tau Alpha Delta Christian Sorority, Inc. in December 2018, and her sorors call her "DeVoted."

Facebook: @Damita Wynn (Dee Sweeney)
Instagram: @Damitalw
Email: damitalwynn@gmail.com
Twitter: @TheWynningTouch

Nyree Fray, MA, LPC, CPCS, originally from Queens, New York, has a master's degree in psychology and an MHA specializing in informatics. She is a licensed professional counselor and certified professional counselor supervisor with over 25 years of experience in behavioral health, addictions, and intellectual developmental disabilities. Her counseling style includes cognitive behavioral therapy, solution-focused with active listening, empathy, and transparency. Currently, Nyree manages a mobile crisis team in metro Atlanta, is employed by Veterans Administration, and provides individual counseling services through a private organization. Nyree joined Tau Alpha Delta Christian Sorority, Inc. in May 2021, and her sorors call her "FreshWind."

Facebook: @NyreeDawnFray
Email: nyreedawnfray@gmail.com

Korean V. Peoples, a native of Southern California, is an author, speaker, and entrepreneur who motivates, inspires, and encourages individuals to rebuild their faith and belief in themselves and Christ. In 2013, Korean unexpectedly became a widow. This new experience was the driving force behind the launch of her nonprofit organization, Women's Think Tank, Inc, whose focus and passion are to help widows rebuild and redefine their lives after suffering an unexpected loss of a spouse. Korean is a mother of two and grandmother of three. Family is her everything, but Jesus is her life. Korean joined Tau Alpha Delta Christian Sorority, Inc. in May 2021, and her sorors call her "In-Power."

Facebook: @korean.peoples
Instagram: @koreanp
Email: Korean4Christ@yahoo.com
Website: www.womensthinktank.weebly.com

Raychelle F. Arnold is from Detroit, Michigan, currently residing in Phoenix, Arizona. She is the founder of Wisdom Heals Sisterhood, Inc., where she is committed to encouraging, motivating, and inspiring women, whether single, divorced, married, or widowed, dealing with challenging issues preventing them from becoming the woman God created them to be. She is a certified growth coach, master encourager, author, and real estate agent. Raychelle is the mother of two adult daughters and loves to travel and entertain family and friends. She joined Tau Alpha Delta Christian Sorority, Inc. in December 2015, and her sorors call her "Resolution."

Facebook: @Raychelle Arnold-Lee
Instagram: @Raychelle Arnold-Lee

Stacie Hayes, Ed. S. earned an educational specialist degree in the helping relationships field of education, now with over 18 years of experience. She is the Founder and CEO of *C-Our-Age In Its Finest,* which is a community that focuses on the power of women, no matter their age. C-Our-Age In Its Finest encourages women to live their "life age" with confidence. She is the author of the guided journal *Friends On In 52*, which is a tool to assist individuals with documenting their gatherings as memory keepsakes, and she is the author of *Alivia And The Tree of Awakening,* a tween book that teaches the lesson that the choices you make today will determine the choices you have tomorrow. Stacie joined Tau Alpha Delta Christian Sorority, Inc. in May 2021, and her sorors call her "Tru-Vine."

Facebook: @stacie.hayes.370
Website: www.couragenif.com

Cherise Lenore Riley was born and raised in Miami, Florida, and currently resides in Dallas, Texas. As a serialprenuer, she is a certified business coach, speaker, and author with 25 years of professional experience as a licensed mortgage lender, real estate agent, and certified bonded credit/budgeting consultant. Cherise founded RileyLenore Enterprise, LLC, The Riley Effect ™, Flip My Legacy, ReCreatingMe, and Legacy-Prenuer Summits ™.

Her passion is to see people tap into their true identity and shed trauma to unlock purpose and destiny to build real generational wealth, emotionally, mentally, physically, and financially. Cherise joined Tau Alpha Delta Christian Sorority, Inc. in May 2021, and her sorors call her "OverComer."

Facebook: @riley.lenore
Instagram: @rileylenore
Email: info@rileylenore.com
Twitter: @cheriselenore
Website: www.rileylenore.com

Made in the USA
Monee, IL
14 July 2022

99663769R00059